Kids' Poems

Teaching Second Graders to Love Writing Poetry

Regie Routman

SCHOLASTIC

NEW YORK • TORONTO • LONDON • AUCKLAND • SYDNEY
MEXICO CITY • NEW DELHI • HONG KONG

for Elizabeth

Acknowledgments

A special thanks to all the wonderful students and teachers in the Shaker Heights, Ohio, City School District who helped make this book possible. In particular I am grateful to teachers Liz Crider, Stephanie Eagleton, Amy Fingerhut, Judy Jindrea, Ellen Rubin, Jennifer Shoda, and Tara Strachan who welcomed me into their classrooms and collaborated in teaching poetry writing. Heartfelt thanks go to Amy Fingerhut for her thoughtful response to the entire manuscript.

I am most appreciative of my insightful editor and friend, Wendy Murray, who has the heart and soul of a poet. Wendy embraced this project with great enthusiasm and sensitivity and followed through on every aspect with great care, respect, and attention to detail. Thanks, too, to Terry Cooper for her enthusiastic endorsement and to Kathy Massaro for her bold, innovative design. Finally, thanks to my husband Frank who lovingly supported the entire project.

Cover and interior design by Kathy Massaro
Cover illustration by Laura H. Beith
Back cover photograph by Kalman & Pabst photo group
ISBN: 0-590-22732-7

Contents

The Kids' Poems

Summary of Instructional Plan for Poetry Writing in Second Grade

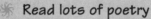

Before you begin

* Read lots of poetry
  * Read poetry aloud
  * Institute "Poet of the Day"
* Establish a poetry corner
* Consider poetry notebooks

Suggested Sequence of Instruction for First Lesson

* What do we already know about poetry?
* Demonstration: Sharing kids' poems and making teaching points
  * Examples of what we notice and discuss
* Writing the first poems
  * Oral brainstorming with students before writing
  * Students writing independently
    * Affirming writers' efforts
    * Capturing the writing "gems"
* Sharing and celebrating

Ongoing, Self-Perpetuating Loop of Instructional Follow-up Sessions (minilessons)

* Sharing and celebrating
* Demonstrating
  * Reading aloud and sharing more kids' poems
  * Shared writing
  * Teacher thinking aloud and writing in front of students
  * Oral brainstorming with students (before students write)
* Writing poems independently
* Capturing gems for minilesson topics

Publishing the Poetry

* Examining anthologies
* Creating an anthology

Why Poetry Writing?

oetry writing is the surest, easiest way I know to turn kids on to writing. Kids love it. Teachers love it. It's fun and easy for everyone (including the teacher). Of all the teaching I do, teaching kids to write poetry has been my favorite and most rewarding experience. Students love playing around with words and patterns in their head and on the page; they love the freedom to write as much or as little as they want; they love that a poem can be about anything at all. They appreciate that fewer words convey the message, and that conventions—while important—loom less prominently. I appreciate all that too, but I especially love that *all* kids are successful.

I first tried free-verse (nonrhyming) poetry writing with second graders several years ago. At the time, I was looking at the kinds of writing we ask kids to do in school and comparing it with the writing I do in my life. I noticed that school writing—mostly journal entries, assignments, and reports—didn't match real-world writing very well. Most of my writing consists of letters, notes, faxes, lists, and, yes, poems. I write free-verse poems for myself, to express my feelings and remember certain happenings, and also to give as gifts to family and friends. Why couldn't young writers do the same? Wouldn't they invest more energy in a form that allowed for maximum choice—not just choice of topic (which they already had in their journals) but choice of form, layout, spacing, pattern, and even conventions? In fact, they could and would use that choice to write with enthusiasm, energy, and quality that often surpassed other writing they did.

Second graders begin to write free-verse poetry with ease and pleasure once they hear, view, notice, and discuss free-verse poems and, in particular, kids' poems—poems by students of similar ages. Seeing lots of poems in original handwriting and invented spellings sends the clear and powerful message to students: "These poems were written by kids just like you. You can do this too."

The message I want to send to you as teacher is the same: *You can do this too.* Initially, it will require a leap of faith to trust the poems themselves and your own judgment to know how and what to teach. It can feel risky to try to teach something where there are no scripted lessons and where kids are given a lot of freedom. But the teaching is easy and structured, the planning is minimal, and the payoff is huge. My hope is to guide you smoothly through the process and give you confidence to begin teaching free-verse poetry writing to your second graders.

Every year I am amazed and delighted to see poetry as the vehicle for turning kids into writers. Kids who don't like to write and who struggle with writing latch onto poetry. Matthew was one such student. He had difficulty staying with any academic task for more than several minutes. His entries in his journals were sparse, and he told everyone that he disliked writing. But something about poetry appealed to him. In this genre, he shone! His first poem (see below) amazed us by its depth, content, length, and effort. Typically Matthew's journal entries were substandard and lackluster. Note a typical journal entry written the day before he wrote his first poem. The difference was astounding and convinced me, once again, that when kids are interested in the task they invest more energy and effort. Not only had Matthew's content improved, his handwriting and spelling were also markedly better. Instead of looking like the poorest, most disinterested writer in the class, he emerged as a student with terrific potential.

Matthew's journal entry, written the day before his inspired poem.

Time

When I get home,

I don't get a chance

To play a game.

When I do homework,

I don't get a chance

To read.

When I get home,

I don't get a chance

To play.

But

When I get home,

Sometimes,

I get a chance to play.

by Matthew McLendon

Once again, free-verse poetry is the best way I know to teach kids how to write easily and joyfully. The unstructured form of free-verse (nonrhyming) poetry with its accompanying possibilities for using phrases and words instead of full sentences seems to make writing easier for kids than more traditional forms. Students learn early on to choose words carefully and to think about language and form. Working in free verse allows all students to have early writing success, and many choose to read and write in this genre throughout the year, both at school and at home. All kids do well: gifted students, reluctant writers, second-language learners, students with learning disabilities, and kids who struggle with the physical act of writing itself. And using kids' poems as models is the most powerful vehicle for this writing success which, in turn, transfers to all other forms of writing students do.

About This Book

You, too, can experience the same success with your second graders and teach every child to write free-verse poems with ease and pleasure; to have fun with language, form, and ideas; to write poems without worry about rhymes; to get thoughts down quickly; to write with a personal style and voice.

Specifically, *Kids' Poems: Teaching Second Graders to Love Writing Poetry* will show you how to:

☀ get started with writing poetry

☀ use kids' poems by other second graders (included in the second half of this book) to inspire and teach budding poets

☀ share and celebrate kids' poems

☀ think aloud and write a poem in front of your students

☀ conduct minilessons—in the context of the whole poem—on many elements of poetry writing, such as: choosing language carefully, experimenting with line breaks (deciding where each line of the poem ends), determining white space (space on page with no words), creating the ending line of a poem, writing with rhythm, and choosing a meaningful topic

☀ write in the style of another poet

☀ create a poetry anthology

Advantages of Writing Poetry

The biggest advantage of teaching poetry writing to second graders is that every child feels competent and successful as a writer. Because they have the freedom and power to express themselves in a format they choose—as well as an environment that supports the process—all children come to love both reading and writing poetry. Some of the best poems, in fact, come from struggling writers.

Poetry writing offers many other important benefits. It:

❋ offers an easy and meaningful alternative to traditional writing forms

❋ extends students' understanding of poetry beyond rhyme to free verse

❋ incorporates all five senses into the writing

❋ encourages kids to play around with language and form

❋ requires fewer words to create a meaningful message which, in turn, helps kids stay focused while writing

❋ extends and supports learning to read

❋ challenges students to be specific and innovative with their use of language

❋ focuses students' thoughts toward selection of vocabulary

❋ frees kids up to write and affirms their writing abilities

Finally, one of the greatest advantages of poetry writing is that kids' voices—their personality and uniqueness—come through in their writing.

Getting Started: Bringing Poetry to the Classroom

ather than relegating poetry writing to a one-time "unit," make it a vital, ongoing part of your reading-writing program. Although you can start teaching poetry any time, I like to begin early in the school year and revisit it again later, while providing opportunities for students to read and write poetry on their own throughout the year. The following sections give you ideas on how to immerse your students in poetry so they will learn to know and love this genre.

Read Lots of Poetry

Create opportunities all year long for kids to hear and read poetry—read poems aloud to the whole class, encourage small group and partner reading of poetry, and offer independent reading time with plenty of poetry choices available. Such exposure and immersion encourages students to enjoy poetry, observe what poets do, and see possibilities for their own writing.

Institute "Poet of the Day"

One quick and easy way to enjoy poetry is to institute "Poet of the Day." Students sign up a day or two in advance to read a favorite poem to the class after lunch or at the end of the day. Or, if students have weekly class jobs, one job can be "class poet." In Amy Fingerhut's class, the class poet reads a poem each day at the end of Drop-Everything-And-Read (DEAR) Time and often chooses to read with a friend or two. In both cases, students practice the poem—written by a student or other published poet—so they can read with fluency and expression (this is great for extra reading practice).

I have found "Poet of the Day" to be particularly powerful in second grade where many readers and writers are in the process of developing and firming up their reading skills and confidence. "Poet of the Day" only takes a few minutes, and all students look forward to this peaceful, enjoyable time. Everyone is successful as a reader.

Establish a Poetry Corner

Designate an area just for poetry, all year long. Bring in your favorite poetry books—from your own collection or borrowed from local libraries—and encourage students to do the same. Include lots of free-verse poetry as well as poems related to science and nature, and whatever subjects your kids are interested in. While there is no one best list of titles to include, one that has been influential for writing quiet poems is *Quiet, Please* by Eve Merriam (Simon & Schuster, 1993). You'll notice several quiet poems by kids in this book. Browse in the children's poetry section of your local bookstore to find your own favorites.

Consider Poetry Notebooks

Try having kids keep a special notebook—or section of their writing notebook—just for poetry. In this space they can write their own poetry and copy their favorite poems by other authors. Having their own work and favorite poems close by makes it easy to go back to memorable wording and encourages kids to reread poems. You may find students memorizing and reciting their favorites, and they can illustrate them too.

Beginning to Teach Poetry Writing

Teaching poetry writing so that all kids are successful requires an in-depth introduction. While the initial session will last about one hour, follow-up sessions may be shorter (50 minutes) as less demonstrating becomes necessary. Don't worry too much about the length of these sessions. Of course, good management is a necessity, but what usually happens is that kids become so engaged that they remain attentive. Still, if the following timeframes seem overwhelming, think about doing the demonstration portion of the lesson in the morning and following later in the day with the remainder of the lesson.

Lesson Framework

Typically, the whole-class format for every poetry-writing session includes:

* **demonstrating poetry writing** (one or two of the following)
  * **sharing, noticing, and discussing kids' poems** (10 to 15 minutes)
  * **teacher writing a poem in front of students** (5 to 7 minutes)
  * **a minilesson on features of poetry** (part of noticing kids' poems)
* **oral brainstorming with students before writing** (5 minutes)
* **writing a poem independently** (20 to 25 minutes)
* **sharing and celebrating** (10 minutes)

For the introductory session only, I limit "demonstrating poetry writing" to "sharing, noticing, and discussing kids' poems," which is one of three possible demonstrations listed in the lesson framework. Also, for the first session and one or more follow-up sessions, I include an informal assessment of what kids know about poetry, which helps guide my teaching (10 minutes). See "What do we already know about poetry?" next page.

What Do We Already Know About Poetry?

For the first introductory lesson and follow-up lessons, gather the class together in the reading area or wherever you usually congregate for whole-class, shared activities. I begin by telling students enthusiastically how excited I am by what we're about to do. I say something like:

> *I am so excited! We've been reading and enjoying lots of poems together. Today we're going to learn how to write poetry, and I know you will love doing it. I will be showing you lots of poems written by second graders just like you. That will help us get started and give you lots of ideas. But before we begin, let's find out what you already know about poetry.*

On a large chart paper I begin to write their responses. When I ask students in Tara Strachan's second grade, "How many of you like to write poetry?" only a few hands go up. When we probe, students give two main reasons why they dislike writing poems, and these responses are typical: *It has to rhyme and that's hard to do* and *I've never done it before.*

However, by the end of our first session, which focuses mostly on enjoying and noticing free-verse poems by other students their age (see pages 15–18) as well as having an opportunity to write, they are wildly enthusiastic. When it is time to stop writing (because they have gym), there are groans.

When we convene again in a follow-up session several days later and I ask them, "What do you know about poetry?" these are their responses, which we list on a chart:

☀ It doesn't have to rhyme.

☀ You can make the poem the shape you want.

☀ You can write about anything.

☀ Your poem can have rhythm.

☀ Put in a title that goes with your poem.

☀ You need to read your poem over to see if it sounds right.

☀ It's important to choose your words carefully.

Eventually, you may want to do a shared writing to make a final chart (once students are very familiar with writing poetry) to serve as a visible guide for poets.

Sharing Kids' Poems and Making Teaching Points

uring this first lesson, we move quickly from talking about poetry to reading and discussing poems by kids. I want to dispel any notions about writing being hard, constrained, or requiring strict conventions. I want kids to write with ease and joy, and seeing kids' poems is the best way I know to accomplish that goal. Or, as one teacher put it, "They don't see themselves as poets till they see other children as poets."

I want students to see and hear immediately that a poem:

※ can be about anything

※ can use few words

※ has a unique form and shape

※ may or may not have rhythm and a beat

※ usually has a title that goes with the poem

※ lets us know the poet

※ is easy to create

※ may be serious or humorous

※ taps into students' interests

※ usually expresses important personal feelings

These poems are written by students just like yours—students who excel in school and students who struggle, students who like to write and students who avoid writing. These are first-draft poems, thoughtfully conceived and quickly written with minimal revision. (You will notice some circled words on some drafts; this occurred later, when students were editing their poems for publication.) These poems are about nature, family, friends, sports, fears, feelings, likes and dislikes—in short, the everyday lives, interests, and concerns of second graders.

I read aloud and show at least five or six kids' poems. First, I say something like the following:

> *Wait until you see the poems I'm going to show you, poems written by other students just like you. These are nonrhyming poems, what we call free verse. They're easier to write than rhyming poems. In fact, most of the poems in the world are written in free verse. I want you to carefully listen to and look at these poems as we enjoy them together. See what you like. See what you notice.*

Until you have your own collection, start with the ones in this book. Kids' poems quickly hook reluctant writers and all writers into believing that poetry writing is doable and pleasurable. Our purpose is for students to discover the fun and joy of writing. And it is the kids' poems by peers that, most of all, provide the confidence and models that spur budding poets into confident action.

Make Poems Visible

Because I want students to see the poems clearly, I usually put them on overhead transparencies. (Feel free to make overheads of your favorites—both the drafts and final copies—from this book.) While you could also gather your class closely together and read aloud the poems and show them to students, being able to easily zero in on individual words and features—and perhaps use an overhead projector pen to point out particulars—makes projected transparencies my first choice.

Discuss the Poem as a Whole

Once again, because I want to instill a love and ease of poetry writing, we primarily enjoy the poems together while discussing the poem as a whole. I have learned from experience that kids easily take in the whole of a poem at once—the title, topic, word choice, line breaks (where the line ends on the page) and white space (space on the page without print), imagery, rhythm, expression of feelings, ending line, and more. Rather than overwhelming students, talking about the poem as a whole seems to help them internalize the essence of poetry as a unique genre.

In the succeeding weeks, we work on the individual elements as necessary (see minilessons, pages 31–36). For example, once students have written a poem they like, we may focus on experimenting with line breaks and white space, editing, titles, word choice—but always in the context of the whole poem.

Keep in mind that there is no formula, no right or wrong way, to read and discuss kids' poems. If you keep your focus on enjoying the poems together, the poem itself will guide you as to what to point out and discuss. The sample classroom conversations on pages 15–18 will give you a feel for how to jump right in and take your cues from the poem. Remember that these kids' poems are mostly simple and straightforward and deal with second graders' interests and feelings. You don't have to worry about deciphering the "right" meaning and elusive language. Once again, the purpose in beginning with kids' poems is to immediately give students lots of energy, enthusiasm, confidence, and ideas for their own writing.

Examples of What We Notice and Discuss

I usually read each poem twice (and sometimes more). Before the first reading I say, "Listen to so-and-so's poem about such and such." I read the poem without commenting and show the student's handwritten draft. Showing the handwritten draft reaffirms the message that a student "just like you" wrote the poem. Seeing the draft also shows that these poems are mostly first drafts with minimal revision. For the second reading, I say, "Listen and look carefully as I read this poem again. What do you notice that the writer has done?" If the draft is easily readable, I show it for the second reading. Otherwise, I display the final copy as I read it aloud so that students can easily follow along.

Here are several examples of how it goes.

Regie: A poem can be about anything at all. Here's one about a favorite sport, "I Like Hockey" [see page 72]. You might want to write a poem about your favorite sport [reads poem draft in original handwriting, using a projected transparency]. I'm going to read Paul's poem again now. Follow along as I read it. Then, we'll talk about what you liked and what you noticed [reads poem again pointing to each word while reading]. What did you like? What do you notice?

Kelly: I like how he says "I love hockey" over and over.

Regie:	Yes, I like that too. He repeats that line. That's something some poets do—repeat some words or lines. It gives the poem a nice beat, a rhythm. Where else does he do that? Look carefully.
Marlon:	He says "I love how…" a few times.
Regie:	Yes, let's look. Give me a line where he says that.
Marlon:	"I love how the skates skim across the slippy, slidy ice."
Regie:	I really like how that sounds. Do you notice something else he does here? What about "skates skim" and "slippy, slidy"?
Tracey:	They all start with *s*.
Regie:	Yes, and even more than that. Listen to how it sounds when you put those s-words together: "skates skim," "slippy, slidy." Paul did that on purpose. He thought about the way he wanted the words to sound together before he wrote them down. The way a poem sounds is part of what makes it a poem. Paul has played around with words here. That's what poets do. Where else does he say "I love how…"?
Devon:	"I love how the puck shoots in full flight."
Regie:	Exactly. And notice how he plays with words here too: "puck shoots in full flight." I love the way that sounds, and I get a vivid picture in my mind, too.
Shelonda:	I like how he says "spider web net."
Regie:	Good noticing. That's a great way to describe the goal pen. I can picture that net because of the words Paul used: "spider web net." Let's enjoy reading the poem together one more time.

I read "Violin Nervous" by Hannah (see page 60).

Violin
Nervous

My violin teacher says,
"You're up."
no, not me
I wish I was sick.
I'm hot pink in the face.
But I do it!

Regie:	Some of you play an instrument and take music lessons. How many of you have ever been in a recital? [Several hands go up.] Listen to this student's experience [reads poem draft]. I love the way the writer tells us exactly how she feels. She lets us know right away with her great title, "Violin Nervous," what her poem will be about. I'm going to read it again. Listen and follow along with me. Notice what she has done [reads draft again]. What do you like? What do you notice?
Jocelyn:	I like how she says, "I'm hot pink in the face but I do it."
Regie:	I love that line too. And I can tell she worked on that. Notice how she's added the word "hot" [points to caret and "hot"]. First she said, "I'm pink in the face." But it didn't sound quite right to her so she changed it to "hot pink in the face." I can see her blushing, nervous face. What else do you notice?
Matt:	She says "I wish I was sick." She doesn't want to play.

Regie: Yes, but then listen to the ending: "But I do it!" Somehow she manages to perform. Her poem isn't long but she's said a lot. I also like how she *shows* us how nervous she is with the words she uses, but she only uses the word "nervous" in her title, not in her poem.

Here's something else to notice. See these line slashes? They are called line breaks, and they show where each line ends. Hannah was thinking about how she wanted her poem to look and sound. The way a poem looks on the page is part of what makes it a poem.

I read "Piano Recitals" by Jenna (see page 58).

Regie: Look at this next poem with me. Notice that Jenna got her idea of what to write about from Hannah's poem, "Violin Nervous," but her poem looks and sounds different from Hannah's. I'm going to read the poem again. Follow along with me [reads poem]. What do you like? What do you notice?

Rasheed: I like how she put "Play! Play! Play!" on the page.

Regie: Yes, I like that too. Why do you think she spread it out like that and made the letters so big?

Rasheed: It's like she's playing the music.

Alaina: She's making it like part of the recital.

Regie: Yes, I think so too. And also, she probably loves playing so much that she gave each word its own line. One of the fun things about writing poetry is that you get to decide exactly how you want your poem to look and sound. You can set it up on the page the way you want, so it makes sense. What else do you notice? How does she let us know how scared she is?

Sydney: She says, "I'm scared head to toe like a shark chasing after me."

Regie: I just love the way she puts that. She doesn't just say "scared;" she tells us her whole body, "head to toe," is scared "like a shark chasing after me." When she says that, we know she's not just scared. It's more like she's terrified. She's chosen her words very carefully to say how she feels. What about the last line?

Patrick: Well she did it. She played and now she's not scared anymore.

Regie: I'm going to read the poem once more. Listen and follow along for how her last line lets us know the poem is over. Last lines are important. When you finish your poem, and as you are writing it, keep rereading it to be sure it looks right and sounds right to you.

I read "Bees" by Colin Duffy (see page 44).

Regie: Here's a fun one by Colin, called "Bees." I love the rhythm of it. I'm going to read it once. Listen and follow along. Then I want you to join in on the second reading [reads poem with lots of expression while keeping the rhythmic beat]. Okay, now read it with me [shows published version]. What do you like? What do you notice?

Tracey: I like how he has "ouch, ouch, ouch" and "buzz, buzz, buzz" and "fuzz, fuzz, fuzz."

Regie: That gives the poem a great rhythm. Repeating words is one way poets create a beat. Let's read the poem just through "fuzz, fuzz, fuzz." Clap the beat as we read it [all read and clap along]. What else do you notice?

Jamaica: I like how he says, "Watch out for flying black and yellow things."

Regie: I like that too. Notice how he placed his poem on the page. When he first wrote his poem [shows draft] he wasn't thinking much about how it would look on the page. It looks like a journal entry. But look at how he then put in line breaks—these slanted lines, called slashes [points to a few]—to show where he wanted each line to end. He read it out loud to himself, and where he stopped his voice, that's where the line ends. When you're writing, think about how you want your poem to look and sound. Keep rereading as you go to check that your poem is just the way you want it.

I continue along in a similar manner with several more kids' poems. Notice that our discussion of elements of poetry has occurred within the context of enjoying the poem as a whole: titles, word choice, layout of poem, line breaks, ending lines, rhythm, repetition and more. This has happened very naturally and easily by listening to and looking at the poems. Even if you have never done this before, you will be successful. Trust your own response to each poem. (For more examples of sharing and noticing specific poems, see pages 32–36.)

The Influence of Peer Poets

The most powerful aspect of reading and discussing poems by other kids of similar ages is the unspoken message these quickly drafted poems send to readers and listeners: "You can do this too." While teacher demonstration is also a strong model (see page 27), the most influential models are the actual poems their peers have written. As you develop a collection of kids' poems to use from year to year (remember to save original drafts and final copies, with kids' permission), you'll find that students delight in recognizing the poems of older siblings and siblings' buddies, as well as poems about familiar school life.

One excellent example of peer inspiration has just been discussed—the influence of Hannah's poem about being nervous at a musical recital on Jenna's choosing to write candidly about a similar experience. Notice the influence of Bethany's lyrical poem about reading, "I'm the Pilot" (see page 76) on Paul's imaginative poem "Reading" (see page 78). It's not just the topic Paul has picked up. He has also been inspired to make highly imaginative comparisons and use figurative language, as Bethany did.

Michael's nature poem, "Hummingbirds," (page 42,) inspired other classmates to write about nature. Note Chanel's poem, "Butterflies"(page 33), Lesley's wind poem (page 48), and Everett's poem "River" on page 46. Second graders are fascinated by natural phenomena, and poetry is a great vehicle to express this interest.

Sometimes teachers worry that a student may imitate another poet's style. However, for some students such imitation initially provides necessary support and structure while learning the craft. Eventually, students feel confident enough to launch their own poetry writing style. Remember, too, that real authors readily cite writers who influence their work.

Writing the First Poems

(20–25 minutes)

Oral Brainstorming With Students Before Writing

(5 minutes)

Oral brainstorming of topics before students begin to write ensures that most students will get started quickly and easily with their own writing. However, when we are just introducing poetry and our sharing and discussing has taken thirty minutes or more as previously described, we may skip oral brainstorming of topics and get directly to writing. This is a judgment call. You want to keep kids' enthusiasm and energy high. With a thorough introductory lesson, most students will have lots of ideas.

For those students who still don't know what to write about (usually, just several students), walk around and briefly conference with them one-on-one to help them get started. Once you have zeroed in on a topic (review the topics of kids' poems shared in the lesson), do some oral brainstorming as modeled below.

For follow-up poetry-writing sessions—after the first one—I usually have kids do some oral brainstorming before sending them off to write. Rather than asking every student what he is going to write about (which is time consuming and allows for only a brief response), I will ask several to talk in detail about what they think they might like to write a poem about. We are still gathered together as a whole class, and with everyone "listening in," I talk with the writer. These one-on-one conversations encourage each student to pursue a topic he is interested in and to think about word choice, beginnings, endings, and so on.

Here are a few examples of how it goes:

Regie:	Who knows what they're going to write about?
Errion:	I'm going to write about monsters.
Regie:	What do you want to say about them?
Errion:	Monsters aren't real. Monsters aren't real.
Regie:	I like the way you repeated that. Everyone, let's say the lines and clap to the beat. [All join in.] What else do you want to say?

See page 68

Errion:	Do you believe in monsters?
Regie:	I like the way you ask a question. Poets do that sometimes. Perhaps you want to answer your question, "Do you believe in monsters?" How would you answer that?
Errion:	"I don't."
Regie:	Let's hear how it sounds so far, Errion. Say it with me,

> *Monsters aren't real.*
> *Monsters aren't' real.*
> *Do you believe in monsters?*
> *I don't.*

	Oh, you've got a good start and a nice rhythm. Do you know what you want to say next?
Errion:	Are you afraid of the dark? I'm not.
Regie:	Okay, good. You seem ready to finish this on your own. Don't forget to keep rereading it to see if it sounds right and looks right, and think about the ending lines. Make sure your poem sounds as if it's ended.

Regie:	Who else knows what they're going to write about?
Chrystal:	My cousin Alexis.
Regie:	What do you want to say about your cousin?
Chrystal:	I'm sad she moved.
Regie:	Oh, that's so hard when someone you like moves. How could you begin?
Chrystal:	My cousin Alexis moved.
Regie:	How did you feel about her?
Chrystal:	I felt like she was my sister.
Regie:	Put that in your poem. What was it like for you when she moved?
Chrystal:	I felt like I was invisible.
Regie:	Wow! That's a powerful line. You're saying exactly how you feel. I'm going to write that on this Post-it™ so you can remember it [puts Post-it on her desk]. What was it like for you when you and Alexis were together?
Chrystal:	We played lots of games together. I was happy.
Regie:	Chrystal, you seem ready to write. Think about how you want your poem to look on the page and how you want your poem to end. Read your poem over and be sure it looks and sounds just the way you want it to.

My Cousin Alexis

My cousin Alexis moved. I felt like she was my sister. When Alexis moved I felt like I was invisible. When Alexis was here I was happy. We played lots of games. I cannot name them. I miss Alexis A lot.

See page 64

Beginning to Write (15 to 20 minutes)

After one or two more similar conversations about topic and word choice, kids begin to write. I tell them something like the following:

> *Write about what really matters to you. Read your poem over to yourself to see if it sounds right. Speak the words aloud softly to yourself so you can really hear how it sounds. Think about how you want your poem to look on the page as you write it. If you finish one poem, start another. Afterwards, those of you who want to share a poem may do so. Have fun writing!*

I also tell students to put their name and date on each poem so we have a permanent record of their work and to skip lines so they have room for changes if they want to make them.

Typically, almost everyone gets to work and easily chooses a writing topic. The quality of even the first poems (many are in this volume) is always a delightful surprise. Students are often much more specific and personal as compared to their journal entries, which are typically about what they did on a particular day. Based on all the models they have seen, students easily grasp that poems are often about things that produce a strong feeling.

Affirming Writers' Efforts

As students begin to write, I circulate about the room, stopping to talk briefly with each student at their eye level. My main purpose here is to encourage, support, and affirm each writer's efforts. The following comments are typical ones that I make during these short chats. Usually, I make one such comment quickly and move on.

* I like that title. I know exactly what your poem will be about.

* I saw you rereading your first few lines. That's what thoughtful writers do.

* You seem to be having trouble getting started. Let's think together about the poems we looked at today. I know you have [a pet] too. You could write about that. I'll help you think about how to begin.

* I like the way your poem looks on the page. I can tell you're thinking about that as you write.

* What an interesting topic. I can't wait to see how your poem turns out.

* I like the words you used. I can picture exactly how you were feeling.

Supporting a Reluctant Writer

As I am moving about the room giving support and affirming writers, I also try to give a boost to anyone who needs it. When a student seems to be having difficulty, I have a brief conversation to get her going. Here's one example:

Regie: Ashley, you seem to be having trouble getting started.

Ashley: (no response)

Regie: You saw and heard a lot of poems today. What's something important to you that you might write about?

Ashley: I don't know.

Regie: Well, what's on your mind? What have you been thinking about?

Ashley: My friend died.

Regie: Oh, I am very sorry. That is so terribly sad. You know, Ashley, a poem is a perfect place to write about that if you feel comfortable doing so.

Ashley: (nods her head)

Regie: Well, your poem doesn't have to be long. Just tell what happened and how you feel. How could you begin?

Ashley: My friend Kenton is dead. He was my best friend.

Regie: What happened?

Ashley: He got hit by a car.

Regie: Just put that in your poem, the way you told me.

See Ashley's completed poem on page 62. Notice her awareness of white space and shape even in her original draft. The line breaks were added later, after a minilesson (see page 35). Notice most of all, with your students, how powerful this poem is for clearly expressing a painful yet important event in her life.

My Friend
Kenton

My friend
Kenton
is dead.
He
was my best friend.
My friend
Kenton
got hit
by a car.

Capturing and Celebrating the Writing "Gems"

During the first poetry-writing session, I listen and look for writing "gems"—those words and phrases that are especially powerful. When a child says or writes one, whether it's during oral brainstorming or while I'm circulating through the room during writing time, I stop and draw everyone's attention to what the writer has done well. I write the gem on a Post-it (as I did for Chrystal above) or I ask the writer to read aloud to the class what he's written. I want students to immediately hear good examples of whole poems, titles, beginning lines, rhythm, sensory words, layout. Instantly congratulating writers for their gems and sharing these with the class builds confidence and gives budding poets ideas and inspiration.

After a student stands in place and reads his writing aloud, I often hold up the poem and read it again. I comment on specific, noteworthy features. For example, after Lesley read aloud the beginning of "A Windy Day" (see page 48 for completed poem), I said

> *What a lovely beginning. I love the way Lesley writes about the wind, "Fast! Faster!! Pushing my jacket back and forth! Knocking my hair onto the smooth skin of my face!" She has made the wind come alive by her careful description and choice of words.*
>
> *And look how Lesley has set her poem up the page. I can tell she's speaking the words to herself and thinking about how the poem will look and sound. Notice how she has "Fast!" and "Faster!!" each on a line by itself.*

This sharing (and noting gems), while students are in the process of writing in a new genre, serves several purposes. It

- ❊ congratulates the writer for her choice of words
- ❊ encourages the writer to continue to carefully consider word choice, shape, title, and so on
- ❊ serves as a model for other students
- ❊ sets expectations for quality
- ❊ reaffirms students' abilities to write poetry

In subsequent writing sessions, once poetry writing is in full swing, I remain on the lookout for gems, but I do not interrupt the writing flow during writing time. Rather, I note the gem on a Post-it and ask the writer to read it aloud during sharing time.

Here are a few more examples of how the process goes:

Regie: Geoff, read your poem on rollerblading (see page 74). I love the way you've set it up on the page with all that movement. Hold it up after you've read it so everyone can see it.

Geoff: [proudly reads poem and displays it.]

Regie: Everett, read your first line of "River" (see page 46).

Everett: River, where do you go with grace and beauty?

Regie: That sounds so beautiful. You have really thought carefully about your choice of words and your topic. And I love the way you ask a question too. I can't wait to see the completed poem.

Regie: Jenny, read us your title and your first few lines (see poem on page 52).

Jenny: The edge of the pond where no fish goes, the edge of the pond where the frogs hang ten.

Regie: I like how you've repeated the beginning of the first line and used your imagination. I can't wait to hear what comes next.

Sharing and Celebrating

After writing time, students who are eager to share do so. Sometimes we gather in a whole-class area. Other times students stand up in place and read their poems. Some days students pair up or read in self-selected, small groups. Because our main purpose in poetry writing is to free kids up to write, to make the process fun and easy, and to give all kids confidence in their abilities as writers, we do not use sharing time to critique. Sharing time is primarily for congratulating and celebrating writer's efforts. Sometimes, students will recognize the superior quality of a poem and break into spontaneous applause. Occasionally, I will quickly point out something the writer has done especially well. But mostly, we just listen to and appreciate each writer's efforts. Sharing time goes quickly. Because poems are seldom more than a page, everyone who chooses to share can do so.

Follow-up Sessions

A fter the first poetry-writing session—as described on the preceding pages—plan to focus on teaching poetry writing a minimum of several days a week, for at least two to three weeks. Such immersion allows lots of time for multiple demonstrations as well as lots of opportunities to write and share poems. During this teaching focus, everyone is expected to be writing poetry. After the teaching focus, writing poems becomes a free-choice writing option.

Poetry writing follows the format of a writing workshop:

* demonstration or minilesson (5 to 15 minutes)
* sustained writing (20 to 25 minutes)
* sharing and celebrating (5 to 15 minutes)

Time allotments will vary and will depend on your purposes. While all aspects of writing workshop are integral to poetry writing, they are not discussed in detail in this book. For a full description, see my book *Conversations: Strategies for Teaching, Learning, and Evaluating* (Heinemann, 2000).

Demonstrating Before Each Poetry-Writing Session
(5 to 15 minutes)

Ongoing demonstrations are necessary to ensure that students have ideas for writing, expectations for quality, an understanding of the elements of poetry so they apply them to their own work, and the knowledge and confidence to write independently.

Demonstration at the beginning of your poetry-writing session may involve one or more of the following, or any combination of these, depending on your purposes:

* sharing and noticing more kids' poems
* the teacher thinking aloud and writing in front of students
* a minilesson on aspects/elements of poetry

Many of these demonstration lessons arise in response to what kids are already doing or attempting to do. Occasionally, teachers include a whole-class, shared writing of a poem as a demonstration. As stated before, enjoying and noticing kids' poems are the most powerful demonstrations.

Sharing and Noticing More Kids' Poems

At the start of the writing session, share several poems by second graders and ask students what they notice. (You may also want to use the poems in *Teaching First Graders to Love Writing Poetry*—for additional models at the beginning of the school year, and *Teaching Third and Fourth Graders to Love Writing Poetry*—for additional models near the end of the school year.)

Use kids' poems to talk about such elements as:

- the importance of titles
- using just the right word to say what you mean
- expressing feelings
- choosing a topic that taps into a personal interest
- creating the rhythm of a poem
- experimenting with line breaks and white space
- crafting the ending line

Regarding what to focus on, take your lead from the poem itself. See minilessons on pages 31–36 for some examples. Even though you will be discussing specific text features, remember to treat each poem as a whole.

Teacher Modeling

Our own thinking and writing, and our willingness to share this process with students, is a powerful model. Even though it may be hard for you to write with your students looking on, take the risk and try it. Your thinking aloud and writing will motivate, inspire, and teach your students.

When I am writing in front of students, I try to keep my poems on a level comparable to what most students are able to do. I choose a topic that resonates for me and that has possible connections for their own writing. Other than considering what I might write about, I do no preplanning for this writing. I want to remain authentic in my demonstration; that is, if I am asking students to write "on the spot," I need to do the same.

One day, early in the school year, I wrote about being forced to eat peas when I was growing up. I chose this topic because:

✳ it's about parents making you do something you don't want to do (a topic everyone can relate to)

✳ I want kids to know you can express your feelings in a poem

✳ I feel very strongly about this topic. (I love all vegetables except peas!)

Here's how I begin:

> *You know, kids, when I was growing up, my parents wouldn't let me leave the table until I'd eaten all my peas. I hated peas and used to swallow them whole rather than chew them. How many of you have had to do something or eat something you didn't like? Well, you can write a poem about that.*

Regie: [sitting on a chair in front of a chart tablet with the class gathered around sitting on the floor] Okay, how do I want to start. Hmm. I think I'll call my poem "Hating Peas" [writes it and thinks out loud]. When I was little I had to eat all my peas. I couldn't leave the table till I'd eaten every last one of them. Okay, I'm going to write that down, see how it looks, and think about where I want the line breaks to go as I'm writing. [Begins to write and says words while writing.]

> *When I was little*
> *I had to eat all my peas.*
> *I hated them!*

I didn't know I was going to add that line, but I really felt strongly about that and still do, so I'm putting an exclamation mark here [continues writing and thinking aloud].

> *I couldn't leave the table*
> *Till I'd eaten every last one of them.*

I'm going to read this from the beginning to see how it sounds [reads from the beginning]. I'm going to change that last line. It doesn't sound right. I think I'll say "I couldn't leave the table [pauses] till my plate was clean" [crosses out last line written and writes *Till my plate was clean*]. That sounds better. Let's see. What do I want to say next. I'm going to read from the beginning. That's what poets do. They reread as they write. I often get ideas on how to continue as I reread [rereads and then writes while speaking aloud].

> *"What's taking you so long?*
> *Hurry up," Mother said.*
> *But I couldn't.*

I continue along in the same fashion, writing on the chart, thinking out loud as I go and rereading, making changes until I'm satisfied. Then I ask the students to read with me.

Hating Peas

(handwritten draft)

Hating Peas

When I was little
I had to eat all my peas
I hated them!
I couldn't leave the table
~~Till I'd eaten every last one of them~~
Till my plate was clean.
"What's taking you so long?)
~~Hurry up.,~~ always
Mother said
"Hurry up." But I couldn't.

Sometimes I sat there
For what seemed like hours .

Finally
After swallowing them whole
My ~~misery~~ agony ended.
I still hate peas today.

Hating Peas

When I was little
I had to eat all my peas
I hated them!
I couldn't leave the table
Till my plate was clean.
Sometimes I sat there
For what seemed like hours
"What's taking you so long?"
Mother always said.
"Hurry up."
But I couldn't.
Finally
After swallowing them whole
My agony ended.
I still hate peas today.

Notice how my poem influenced Faith to write about her own distasteful experience eating peas (see "Peas," page 54). In front of second graders, I have also written poems about my dog, the influence of my grandmother on me, friends, family, favorite foods, being nervous before I talk in front of a lot of people, and many other real-life topics.

Writing in the Style of Another Poet

I like using *Baseball, Snakes, and Summer Squash: Poems About Growing Up* by Donald Graves (Boyds Mills Press, 1996) for opening up additional writing possibilities for students—topics, style, word choice, layout and more. In free verse, Graves writes about what it was like when he was a kid: his first girlfriend, hating certain vegetables, his dog, giggling in church, and being teased, to name several topics. For our demonstration in one follow-up session, I read several of these poems aloud and ask students, "What do you notice?" We talk about how Graves writes about everyday subjects, and we notice that Graves:

☀ puts himself in the poem

☀ tells how he feels

☀ uses conversation

☀ includes details

☀ uses humor

☀ makes his poem sound like a story

After I demonstrate by writing a poem myself (see "Hating Peas" on pages 28–29 for one such example), I expect everyone to try writing in the style of Graves. Be sure you model one such poem yourself. Your own willingness to risk and write openly about an embarrassing moment, difficulty, or something you feel strongly about, sends the message to students that poetry can be used to express feelings about important moments and events. When one teacher wrote about being embarrassed that her ears stuck out, several students wrote about similar feelings of embarrassment—being short, being clumsy, losing things. See Anthony's poem (above) for his honest expression of a quiet confrontation with his mom.

Skipping Chores
By Anthony Hall

One night when I came
home from school
My mom said
"you skipped your chores."
I did not answer
She said
"you march up to your room."

Use the poems in this volume to spur your students to write honestly and in the style of Graves (or another favorite poet). Besides "Peas," on page 54, read, notice, and discuss "Curly Fries" by Jasmine (see page 56) who uses poetry to express dislikes and hurt feelings. Notice, again, the previously discussed poems "Piano Recitals" (page 58) and "Violin Nervous" (page 60). See, also, "Summertime" by Allen (page 40) who closely observes and narrates going swimming at a pool with Mom and Grandpa and makes it all come vividly to life. Allen also uses conversation and a refrain, "'Don't get me wet!' says Mom," to spotlight Mom's typical behavior.

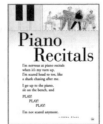

Minilessons

Minilessons are delineated on the following pages only to illustrate some possibilities for poetry writing and discussion. Keep in mind that the purpose is not to break a poem into skills or parts but to strengthen the quality of your students' poems and to increase writing possibilities for them as well.

In "Examples of What We Notice and Discuss," on pages 15–18, each discussion of a poem focuses on specific elements, but always in the context of the whole, meaningful poem. For example, when noticing and discussing Paul's poem, "I Like Hockey," we talk about topic, repeating words, rhythm, playing around with words, and noticing how words sound together—all at once. And again, when discussing Hannah's poem, "Violin Nervous," we talk about the title, choosing words carefully to express a feeling, making a change to get a line "just right," line breaks, the ending line, rereading to make sure the poem looks and sounds right—all while enjoying the poem together.

When you are pointing out features of a poem, just look at each poem and see what you notice. What you focus on will evolve naturally from what the writer has done. Even if you have never done this before, you will be successful. Remember to look at the poem as a whole and keep the focus on making poetry writing easy, pleasurable, and successful for your students. Use the poems in this book as well as the poems your own students write.

Choosing Topics

Encourage your students to write about what really interests them—what they care about, what they know, what they observe, how they feel about things. Use the topics of the kids' poems in this volume as a resource for ideas. My experience has been that second graders will write memorable poetry as long as they can choose the topic. When one second grade teacher told her students that they all had to write a Thanksgiving poem, the results were deadly. The kids labored for three days, prodded and encouraged by the teacher, but the poems were decidedly lackluster. When she returned to self-selection of topics, quality and interest soared.

That doesn't mean you can't require students to write certain kinds of poems, as I demonstrate in the lesson on *Writing in the Style of Another Poet* (page 30). The difference here is that the choice of topic remains with the students.

Small Poems

I want students to know that poems can be short, that poets choose their words carefully, and that you don't have to write a lot to be descriptive. I make sure that I share small poems with students, and I ask them to try their hand at these. I model writing a short poem (see "Liz," below) and share small poems by other students. Many poems in this book are small poems. See Vicki's delightful poem, "Rain," below.

Notice William's "The Shower is a Special Place," on page 50, where in just eighteen words he views the shower as a waterfall. See "All My Friends" by Anthony on page 66 and notice how Anthony focuses mostly on naming his friends and writes a rhythmic, uncomplicated poem.

Liz

Soft brown hair
Shiny, tumbling
Fingers moving across forehead
Spreading wisps away.

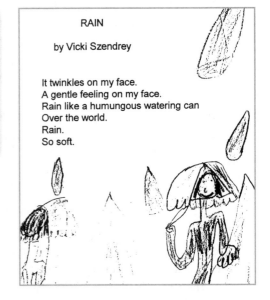

RAIN

by Vicki Szendrey

It twinkles on my face.
A gentle feeling on my face.
Rain like a humungous watering can
Over the world.
Rain.
So soft.

Choosing Language Carefully

Careful word choice can create images, moods, and depth in a poem. Here are a few more examples to spark observation and discussion.

"Hummingbirds" by Michael on page 42. Michael masterfully uses detailed airborne images and sensual, earthy ones to beautifully describe hummingbirds. You might want to note the poet's intense and lyrical observation including his simile (a comparison using *like* or *as*), "like holograms" and his metaphor (a comparison without *like* or *as*), "Their tiny feathers a train." Talk about how Michael has made every word count.

* "Rollerblading" by Geoff on page 74. Kids love saying this poem where each word is emphasized on its own.

* "Butterflies" by Chanel Miller. See below. Note the artfulness and cadence of her phrases, the careful observation, and the simile, "like butter on bread."

Chanel Miller

Badfit

Badfitis g et weis
srag in the aer
Like baed on bred
the siet wei's
aive a baebfli
the swit dalors

Butterflies

Butterflies quiet wings
spreading in the air
like butter on bread
The silent wings
of a butterfly
The sweet colors

Notice, too, that if we look only at Chanel's spelling, she would be labeled a struggling writer or low-achieving student. When we look at her language facility, she is gifted. Poetry writing—with its initial de-emphasis on the mechanics of handwriting, spelling and punctuation—has facilitated her ability to express herself freely and poetically.

Ending Lines

Beyond what has already been discussed throughout these pages, here are several poems to use for focusing on ending lines:

* "Curly Fries" by Jasmine on page 56. Notice how she capitalizes many words for special emphasis and how her ending line brings closure.

- "I'm the Pilot" by Bethany on page 76. Talk about how she uses the ending line "All in my room reading" to surprise the reader and let us in on what the poem is really about.

- "River" by Everett on page 46. Discuss how the last lines ask a question: "But where do you go, mighty river? Where do you go?" and reiterate the poet's unending curiosity about a natural phenomenon.

 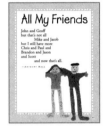

- "A Windy Day" by Lesley on page 48. Her last line, "The invisible creature has gone away" shows personification, changes the pattern of the language, and brings sophisticated closure.

- "All My Friends" by Anthony on page 66. Read the poem without his ending line "and now that's all" and note how the poem doesn't sound complete without it. Talk about how the last line also connects to earlier lines "but that's not all" and "but I still have more."

Repetition

Repeating words, phrases and lines can increase the impact of a poem, as has been previously discussed. Here are a few more examples of repetition:

- "Summertime" by Allen on page 40. Talk about how repeating the lines "Don't get me wet!" three times gives the poem a comfortable rhythm and also reminds us that all moms are like this!

- "Hummingbirds" by Michael on page 42. Notice the beautiful structure his repetition of "Hummingbirds," (followed on next line by) "see" sets up.

- "Storm" by Carolyn on page 70. Her repetition of "Oh" four times as well as her repeated use of different sounds of thunder and rain give this poem a delightful rhythm.

✳ "Birds" by Ronnie Taylor (below). Notice how he begins and ends the poem in a similar way, which helps give the poem its graceful pattern and rhythm. This poem has an easy and appealing structure for kids to model or adapt.

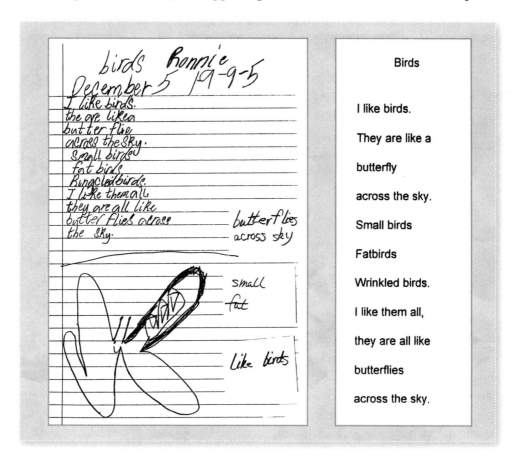

Birds

I like birds.

They are like a

butterfly

across the sky.

Small birds

Fatbirds

Wrinkled birds.

I like them all,

they are all like

butterflies

across the sky.

Line Breaks and White Space

Line breaks help to set the rhythm of the poem as well as to create the white space and shape of the poem. The way the poem looks and sounds is what makes it a poem and differentiates it from other forms of writing. As you look through kids' poems with your students, notice the many different ways students have arranged their poems on the page: from one or two words on a line to two-to-five line stanzas (arrangement of a certain number of lines).

It's been interesting to observe that young writers do not have difficulty understanding and applying the notion of line breaks and white space. In examining more than one hundred drafts of poems by second graders, I find most of them are written on the page with the shape of the poem (created by the line breaks) evolving during the original writing. Note that this statement is true for the majority of poems included in this book. I believe that students easily grasp the notion of line breaks and white space because they have heard, seen, noticed, and discussed many poems together before attempting to write on their own.

However, when a student or students have written without line breaks, as Faith did in "Peas" on page 54 and Chrystal did in "My Cousin Alexis" on page 64, I teach them how to think about and apply the line breaks. Most often, I will say something like:

Think about how you want your poem to sound and to look on the page. I'm going to read your first line. Do you want it to sound this way [reads with break in one place] or this way [reads with break in a different place]? Should we end it here [points to word] or here [points to word]? Which way sounds better to you? Put your line break there.

With the student's permission, I will put her poem without line breaks (or I use a former student's poem) on an overhead transparency. I'll read the first lines several times, each time pausing in a logical but different place so the student hears and sees the different possibilities. Then I ask where I should place the line break(s), and I read it again to be sure that it sounds good to the student. Once the student seems comfortable, I stop and let her take over on her own.

A caution about line breaks: Don't worry about line breaks until kids are editing favorite poems. While I model line breaks all along and we talk about it in the context of noticing and discussing kids' poems (as noted in these pages), I don't emphasize line breaks until later. And even then I continually remind kids that line breaks are up to them—as free-verse poets, they can set up the lines however they wish. I want to keep kids focused on the joy of expressing themselves freely in a poem.

Publishing the Poetry

Almost all students word-process or handwrite at least one favorite poem after getting it into final form. I usually expect students to write several poems over the course of our poetry writing and then choose a favorite for publication in the anthology. During sustained writing time, once students have revised their chosen poem and edited it (perhaps with a peer), I have a final editing conference with each student. Since the poems are rarely more than a page long—and often less—these conferences go quickly. Also, because students have chosen their poem's format, the usual burden for exactness in capitalization and punctuation—although these remain important—is eased somewhat, causing all students to invest seriously in the editing process.

Examining Anthologies

As part of one of our demonstration sessions, I begin by asking students if they know what an anthology is. Typically, they do not know. I show them several poetry anthologies, some commercially published and others written and organized by students from previous years. I flip through these anthologies and comment on the dedication, contents, index, poet profiles, illustrations, and the organization of each anthology. (Once I have anthologies by students, I include these too.) With prompting and guidance, students determine that a poetry anthology is a collection of poems. Examining anthologies can take place any time before publishing. Sometimes we talk about anthologies as part of our introductory session (following "What do we already know about poetry?"). Sometimes, we wait till we're getting ready to publish.

In any case, let your students know that they will be creating a classroom anthology with one or more poems from every student. Give them at least several days or more to look through and enjoy reading the poems in the anthologies, both student-made and commercial, that you place in your poetry corner. (Sustained silent reading time works well for exploring these.) Tell students to be thinking about how they want their own classroom anthology to look and be organized.

Creating an Anthology

Kids love having a classroom anthology to call their own and show off their hard work. Once students have had sufficient time to examine anthologies, decide together what the content and organization of their anthology will be. Then brainstorm possibilities for what their anthology will include. I ask students, "What did you notice about the anthologies you looked at?" What follows are the observations from one brainstorming chart created in a shared writing with second graders:

- [ ] a lot of different poems by different authors
- [x] acknowledgments—at front or back—give thanks to those that helped
- [ ] index at back—can be titles, authors, first lines, subjects
- [x] contents at front—title of poem, author, page format—whole page, columns
- [x] title page
- [ ] introduction or About This Book section
- [x] illustrations—format—two pages for each poem, can use colored pencils
- [x] dedication
- [ ] back cover
- [ ] About the Poets page
- [ ] writing of poems—word processed
- [x] title
- [x] cover

Pets
by Nozomi Mori

I like pets.
I don't have pets,
but pets are pretty.
I like dogs and cats
and rabbits and
hamsters and mice.
I like birds and cardinals.
I like pets!

The anthology you and the students create can be as simple or complex as you decide. Some teachers have each student bring one poem to final copy, usually with an accompanying illustration. These are bound simply into a classroom book, and each student gets a treasured photocopy to read and keep. Other classes go to elaborate lengths to produce a beautiful anthology, and many include an "About the Poet" page (from the teacher too) to go along with each poem. Note the checkmarks on the above list indicating that class's final decisions about what their anthology would include.

Once you have a student anthology, it serves as a wonderful model for future students. Second grade teacher Jennifer Shoda notes how her new class responds each year: "The reaction is always so powerful. The anthology really grabs the kids. When they read other kids' poetry, it really hits home. It shows students what's possible."

Closing Thoughts

Writing free-verse poems is a liberating experience for many second graders. Unencumbered by demands for strict form and exacting conventions, an amazing sensitivity, awareness, and strong personal style emerge. Students' fascination with the natural world, their powers of observation, their ability to evoke emotion and a particular mood and tone all come through in their poetry writing. Even the students who usually struggle with writing write freely, imaginatively, and joyfully. As Jennifer Shoda notes,

Poetry writing is an amazing way for writers who struggle to succeed. To come up with a whole story is overwhelming. With poetry, all of a sudden, they're not so worried about writing, and the poems they write are so wonderful.

The students say it best. When Ellen Rubin's second graders put together their classroom anthology, each student wrote a handwritten, personal statement before his or her published poem. Scott wrote, "I think to write a poem brings joy to all and makes you feel better when you're sad." Vicki wrote, "I like to write poems because poems to me are like a gentle breeze from the wind." Judy wrote, "Writing poems are like a box of treasure I keep in a special place in my room. I open the box when I feel alone and sad." One parent wrote, "We are so delighted he was introduced at a young age to poetry."

Good luck and much success with the treasures your own students will uncover and create. You and your students are in for a treat. Relax, enjoy, and savor reading and writing kids' poems. All of your students will shine as writers. And the poems your own students create will become your most powerful models of all.

Summertime

Splash, splash   gose water guns
"don't get me wet"   says   mom
* * *
we go to the pool
    grandpa comes too
we get my bathing sut on
* * *

grandpa throths me in
I go SPLASH
    "don't get me wet" mom says
    mom puts on suntan loshen
    I   jump in agen
    "don't get me wet" mom says
    we   go home

—BY ALLEN LOUIS ECKHOUSE

Summertime

Splash, splash go water guns.
"Don't get me wet!" says Mom.

* * *

We go to the pool,
Grandpa comes too
We get my bathing suit on.

* * *

Grandpa throws me in.
I go "SPLASH!"
"Don't get me wet," Mom says.
Mom puts on suntan lotion.
I jump in again.
"Don't get me wet," Mom says.

We go home.

—ALLEN LOUIS ECKHOUSE

HumingBirds

HumingBirds   Michael MᶜIntosh
See there wings
Like Holograms
HumingBrids
See there   ther tiney fethers a train
Sparkling   simbil of puody
fragl ting Bodey
all in the riant forest sucing the jusee necter
from a flower

—BY MICHAEL MCINTOSH

Humming Birds

Hummingbirds
see their wings
like holograms
their tiny feathers a train
symbol of purity
Hummingbirds
see their
sparkling
fragile tiny bodies
all in the rain forest
sucking the juicy nectar
from a flower.

— MICHAEL MCINTOSH

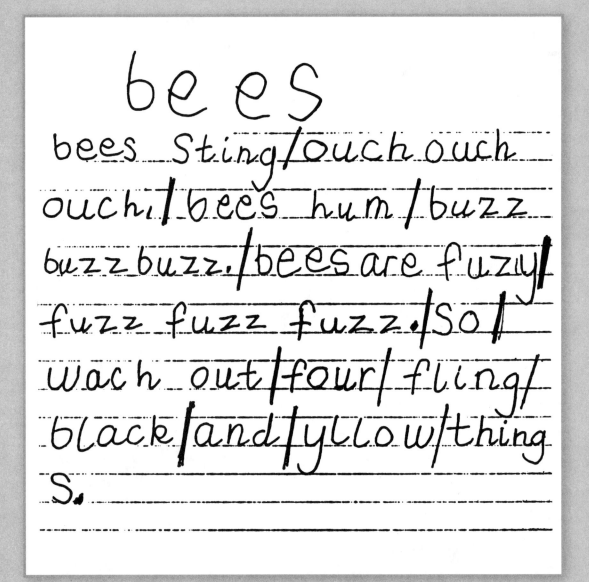

bees

bees sting / ouch ouch ouch. / bees hum / buzz buzz buzz. / bees are fuzzy / fuzz fuzz fuzz. / so / wach out / four / fling / black / and / yllow / things.

—BY COLIN DUFFY

44

Bees

Bees sting
Ouch ouch ouch
Bees hum
Buzz buzz buzz
Bees are fuzzy
Fuzz fuzz fuzz
So
watch out
for
flying
black
and
yellow
things.

— COLIN DUFFY

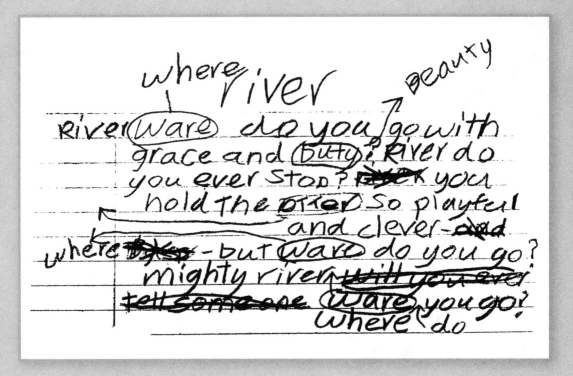

—BY EVERETT HOFFMAN

River

River
Where do you go
with grace and beauty?
River, do you ever stop?
You hold the otter
so playful and clever.
But where do you go, mighty river?
Where do you go?

—EVERETT HOFFMAN

A Windy Day

The Wind is blowing
Fast!
Faster!!
Pushing my jacket
Back and forth!
Knocking my hair
onto the smooth skin
of my face!
pushing my body
to the left
then the right!
Then Silence
absolute silence
the invisible creature
has gone away

—BY LESLEY RAY

A Windy Day

The wind is blowing
Fast!
Faster!!
Pushing my jacket
Back and forth!
Knocking my hair
    onto the smooth skin
    of my face!
pushing my body
to the left
    then the right!
Then Silence
    absolute silence
The invisible creature
has gone away.

—LESLEY RAY

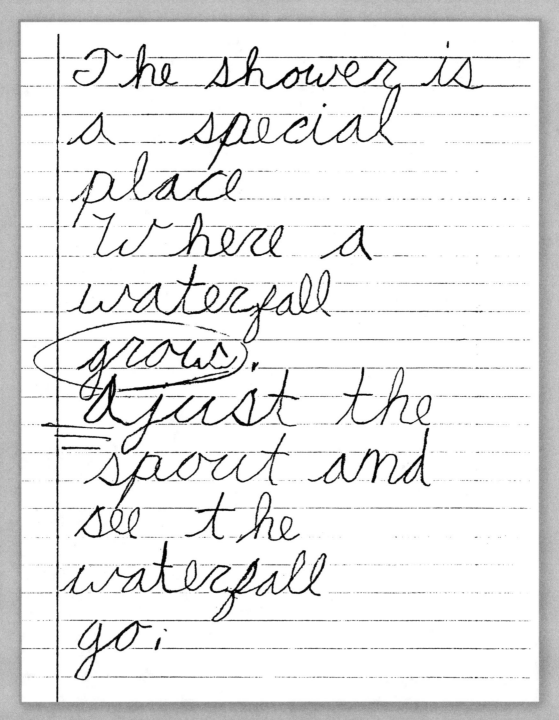

The shower is
a special
place
Where a
waterfall
~~grows~~.
A just the
spout and
see the
waterfall
go.

— BY WILLIAM THOMPSON

The Shower Is a Special Place

The shower is
a special
place
where a
waterfall
grows.
Adjust the
spout and
see the
waterfall
go.

— WILLIAM THOMPSON

the ~~Ege~~ *edge* of The Pond

The ~~ege~~ *edge* of the ~~pond~~ *ponde*
~~Waer~~ *where* no fish ~~goes~~ *goes*

The ~~ege~~ *edge* of the ~~pond~~ *ponde*
~~Waer~~ *where* the frogs ~~hage~~ *hang*
ten/. The ~~ege~~ *edge* of T.he
~~pond~~ *ponde* ~~Waer~~ *where* the ~~Pinses~~ *princess*

~~Kissd~~ *Kissed* the frog/ and

~~Howe~~ *who* Rnows what
will hapin *happan* next! ~~the~~
~~ege of the pond next!~~

at the edge of the
pond /

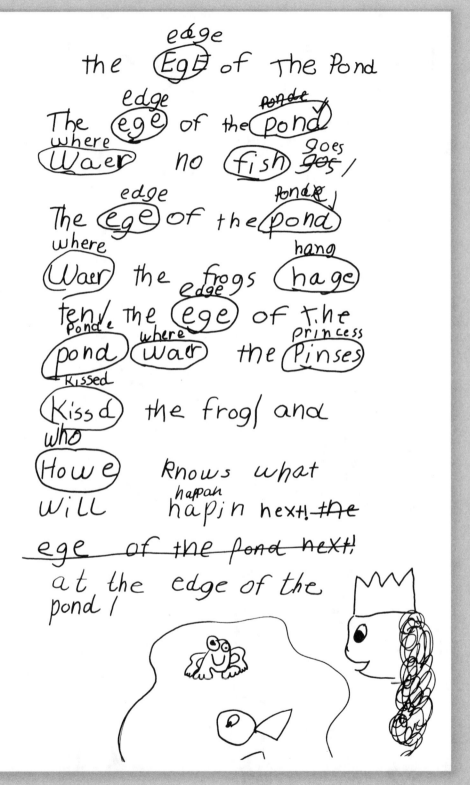

—BY JENNY KUTIK

The Edge of the Pond

The edge of the pond
　　where no fish goes
The edge of the pond
　　where the frogs hang ten
The edge of the pond
　　where the princess kissed the frog and

Who knows what
　　will happen next
at the edge of the pond!

—*JENNY KUTIK*

Faith

Peas

time to eat diner my
moter says I say what
are we hareing she say peas
an rice an chkin I allmost
fanted peas I said mom brings
my plat in an about 10

spons fulls of peas a look
at the desasting green
disgusting
dry ogly monsters jumping in
to my moth disasing wite
disgusting
insids of a pea it is time
to tack ure bath my moth said
I say finlly

—BY FAITH HUDSON

Peas

"Time to eat dinner," my mother says
I say, "what are we having?"
She says, "peas and rice and chicken."
I almost fainted.
"Peas," I said.
Mom brings my plate in
And about 10 spoonfuls of peas.
I look at the disgusting green dry ugly monsters
Jumping into my mouth,
Disgusting white insides of a pea.
"It is time to take your bath," my mother said.
I say, "Finally."

—FAITH HUDSON

CURLY FRIES!

I HATE WHEN
Vaugh calls me "CURLY
FRIES"!
I say "be quiet."
Then the other boys
 call me "CURLY FRIES"!
I feel so mad
That I could
Punch Them In Their
Stomach!
I HATE IT
 WHEN THEY
 CALL ME THAT!

—BY JASMINE RIPPY

Curly Fries!

I hate when
Vaughn calls me
"CURLY FRIES!"
I say, "Be quiet."
Then the other boys
call me
"CURLY FRIES!"
I feel so mad
that I could
punch them in their
stomachs!
I HATE IT
WHEN THEY
CALL ME THAT!

—JASMINE RIPPY

Piano Recitels

I'm nervous at piano recitels
when its my turn up,
I'm scared head to toe Like
a shark chasing after me

I go up to the piano
sit on the bench and,

PLAY!

PLAY!

PLAY!

I'm not scared anymore

—BY JENNA STAHL

Piano Recitals

I'm nervous at piano recitals
when it's my turn up,
I'm scared head to toe, like
a shark chasing after me.

I go up to the piano,
sit on the bench, and

PLAY!
    PLAY!
        PLAY!

I'm not scared anymore.

— JENNA STAHL

Violin
nevus

My Violin teacher

Saids "your up"/

no not me

I wish I was

               Hot
sick / I'm ✓ pink

in the face /

But I do it !/

—BY HANNAH CLAIR T'KINDT

60

Violin Nervous

My violin teacher says,
"You're up."
no, not me
I wish I was sick.
I'm hot pink in the face.
But I do it!

—HANNAH CLAIR T'KINDT

My Friend kenton

My friend/

kenton/is

dead/He/is was

my best friend/

My friend/

kenton/got

hit/by

a car.

—BY ASHLEY HICKS

My Friend Kenton

My friend
Kenton
is dead.
He
was my best friend.
My friend
Kenton
got hit
by a car.

—ASHLEY HICKS

cousin

my ~~couser~~ Alexis

my ~~coun~~ attacs

Alexis

my cousi~~n attacs~~, moved.

I felt/like she was my

sister/ when alexis moved

I, felt like I was in visible ~~invibltot~~

when alexis was here

I was Happy /we played,

lots of games I can/

not name them I miss

alexis a lot

—BY CHRYSTAL YARBROUGH

My Cousin Alexis

My cousin Alexis
moved. I felt
like she was my sister.
When Alexis moved I
felt like I was invisible.
When Alexis was here
I was happy.
We played
lots of games.
I cannot name them.
I miss Alexis
A lot.

— CHRYSTAL YARBROUGH

All my Friends

John and Geoff
But that's not all

Mike and Jacob
But I still have more

chris and Paul and
Brandon and Jason
and scott

and now that's
all.

—BY ANTHONY HALL

All My Friends

John and Geoff
but that's not all
      Mike and Jacob
but I still have more
Chris and Paul and
Brandon and Jason
and Scott
      and now that's all.

—ANTHONY HALL

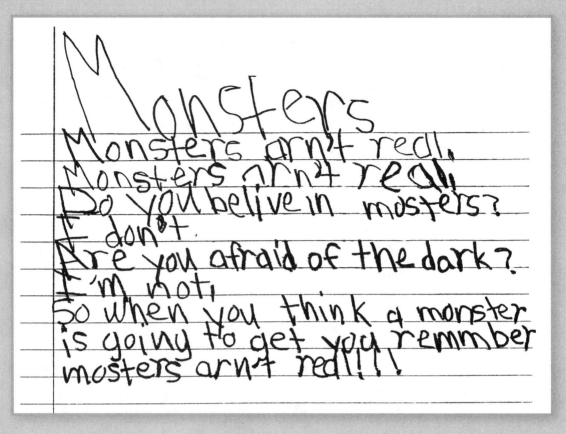

Monsters

Monsters arn't real,
Monsters arn't real,
Do you belive in mosters?
I don't.
Are you afraid of the dark?
I'm not.
So when you think a monster
is going to get you remmber
mosters arn't real!!!

—BY ERRION L. TYREE

Monsters

Monsters aren't real.
Monsters aren't real.
Do you believe in monsters?
I don't.
Are you afraid of the dark?
I'm not.
So when you think a monster
is going to get you, remember
Monsters aren't real!!!!

—ERRION L. TYREE

Storm

Boom
crash
oh, Im
scared
Pitter
Pat
Pitter
Pat
oh
that's
better
Boom
crash
oh
just dont
stort
up again
oh, I
hate thunder
and lightning

—BY CAROLINE HAWES

Storm

Boom
crash
oh, I'm
scared
Pitter
pat
pitter
pat
oh
that's
better.
Boom
crash
oh
just don't
start
up again.
Oh, I
hate thunder
and lightning.

—CAROLINE
HAWES

I like hokey

I Love hockey

l Love how the

Skates skim across the slippy

slidy ice

I Love hockey

I Love how the puck

Shoots in Full flicte

l Love hockey

l Love how the puck

get tangld in the

Spider web net

— BY PAUL A. SKERRY

I Like Hockey

I love hockey
I love how the
Skates skim
Across
The slippy
slidy ice.
I love hockey
I love how the puck
Shoots in full flight.
I love hockey
I love how the puck
Gets tangled in the
Spider web net.

—*PAUL A. SKERRY*

geoff RollerBladeing

frst tight turns

quick speed skates

starap it tight were going

for a ride

zzz z z z z z z z
zo o o ooo ooo ooo oo
oo o o ooo oo ooo oo
oo o o oo ooo oo ooo
oo ooo o o oo oo oo ooooom

—BY GEOFF GOSS

Rollerblading

Fast
    tight
       turns
Quick
    speed
       skates
Strap
    it
      tight
       we're
for
        going
   a
    ride

ZZZZZZZZZZZZZZZZZZZZZZZZZZZZZ
ZOOOOOOOOOOOOOOOOOOOOO
OOOOOOOOOOOOOOOOOOOOOOO
OOOOOOOOOOOOOOOOOOOOOOOO
OOOOOOOOOOOOOOOOOOOOOOOOM

— GEOFF GOSS

Im
the Pilit of a aPLan
the caPd of a Bot
IM
the Brd of the Sci\
OL in my Room Ridin
Bethany

—BY BETHANY WOLFF

I'm The Pilot

I'm
the pilot of an airplane
the captain of a boat
I'm
the bird of the sky
All in my room reading.

— B E T H A N Y   W O L F F

Reading

When I read,

I sove/ (soar)

Over mouting/ (mountians)

By the seas,/

I ride on a fish,/

Through the open waves/

I ride the R.M.S. Titantic (tindtic titan)

I swim in the waves/

I dive in rippily/ (rippley) Lake water

Swimming, Diving, Flying,

Riding/ all, trough my

Reading./

—BY PAUL FRANCIS GRAY

Reading

When I read,
I soar
Over mountains
By the seas
I ride on a fish
Through the open waves.
I ride the R.M.S. Titanic
I swim in the waves
I dive in ripply lake water
Swimming, Diving, Flying, Riding,
All through my reading.

— PAUL FRANCIS GRAY

Illustration Credits

Page 41: Katie B. Kinkel; *Page 43:* Catherine Kelly Licina;
Page 45: Chris McFarlane; *Page 47:* Julia Rooney;
Page 49: Chelsey Lindaya Baker; *Page 51:* Jayson Douglas;
Page 53: Katie B. Kinkel; *Page 55:* Chelsey Lindaya Baker;
Page 57: Gabrielle R. Hughley; *Page 59:* Anna Conley;
Page 61: Sarah G. Van Tassel; *Page 63:* Crystal A. O'Neal;
Page 65: Gabrielle R. Hughley; *Page 67:* Shpresa Kukaj;
Page 69: Armond Banks; *Page 71:* Eva Hoffman; *Page 73:* Evan D. Bates;
Page 75: Anthony Richard Amaddio; *Page 77:* Kevin Gramlich;
Page 79: James Phelan

Thanks also to:

Sarah G. Van Tassel, Ashley P. Hudson, DeAndre Fitten,
Isaac David Zhukovsky